CW01024836

0315

B. Mayr

XL5 EDITIONS

RUSTBOY
(re) **Animating a Lifelong Dream**
by Brian Taylor

First Published in 2003
by XL5 Editions
Dundee
Scotland

www.rustboy.com

Book design by Brian Taylor © 2003
Design, layout, typesetting and production by
Douglas Mullen.

Printed by Nevisprint Limited
Unit 3 Caol Industrial Estate
Fort William
Inverness-shire
PH33 7PH

ISBN 0-9545872-0-0

In memory of my Father and Mother

RUSTBOY

(re) ANIMATING *a* LIFELONG DREAM

Brian Taylor

CONTENTS

INTRODUCTION

In some ways it's a coming-of-age story. A story about the adventures of a little round-headed metal boy. And of a not-so-little Scottish boy, too. About how the Scottish boy dreams up the metal boy and shows him to everyone. And how everyone watches as a world unfolds, idea by idea, piece by piece, pixel by pixel.

Brian Taylor's Rustboy started with a simple, enigmatic trailer for a movie that hadn't been made. And the web, being what it is, reacted with amazing force. The site was linked and cross-linked and discussed and analyzed and what was initially a personal, experimental project immediately became the property of thousands of people who were hungry for details and explanations and more sneak peeks at the material. This is where things got interesting. Because there weren't any more details. There wasn't much to explain and there was virtually nothing more to peek at. Brian's idea was to make this movie himself, alone. No matter how long it took, he'd work in public and allow people to watch his progress on the web.

Maybe it's not so much 'coming-of-age,' but more like 'coming-of-an-age.' Where the technical barriers to the execution of an idea, no matter how big, dense or convoluted, fall away and an individual's vision can become a reality. In as much as the world of any two-foot, partially oxidized, well-mannered robot boy can become a reality.

Now there's no doubt that Rustboy himself generated a lot of interest. His big eyes and infant-like innocence are hard to resist, but the backstory has captured peoples' imaginations as much as anything else. The idea that a single guy, armed with a Mac and some standard-issue 3D software, could produce a movie that would look every bit as good as the latest Hollywood CGI offerings, and base it on a quirky design idea, which is about as far removed from audience research and demographic analysis as possible, is a great story by itself. How could you not root for this to work?

The whole model for the creation of an animated feature, or any movie for that matter, has been completely upended. The coming attractions and the merchandise and the action-figure can come first. This book, which in the regular universe, would be released into bookstores at approximately the same time the movie went into theaters and the toys into Happy Meals, can be published, in Rustboy's universe, well before the movie is complete. The 'special features' can come before the DVD. If you buy into the old chestnut 'the journey is more important than the destination,' then you'll see that there is great satisfaction to be had in investing one's interest in a project and watching it develop over time.

On the scale of man-hours to completion, a movie is a massive task and a book like this only a bit less so. I suppose that people purchase 'The Making of...' books to examine the nitty-gritty details, or to see behind the scenes and appreciate the tricks of the trade. There's some of that here, but of greater

interest is the ability to visually chart the development of the idea, represented by the Rustboy character, from initial sketches, to animation tests through full-blown scenes.

Brian was originally going to title this book 'Jumping in the Deep-End' as a way to explain that a simple idea like, 'Hey, I know, I'll make a little movie about this Rustboy fellow,' can turn into an incredibly complicated obsession. And the deeper you go the more there is to learn and the bigger the task becomes. So he's not really a film-maker but he's making a film. As long as he's not a publisher either, he might as well publish a book. What's next? Brian's not a brain-surgeon, but...

From my perspective, this whole Rustboy enterprise is organized like the spokes of a wheel. Right in the center you'll find Rusty and Brian. Ideas and executions radiate outward and that's where we intersect with them, where with careful planning and long hours they become real. It's probably safe to say that our collective interest in the project, as evidenced by site traffic, emails, magazine and web articles etc., is at least as responsible for it going forward as Brian's individual obsession. And that's what is unique about all this. Being a part of the process, we all have a vested interest in its conclusion and success. Ultimately it's 'our' one guy, one Mac and one idea that keeps growing and maturing.

I don't know about anyone else but I'm a sucker for a story like this. I feel strangely protective of the little guy too. Like I'm his American uncle or something. I don't have the foggiest idea what adventures await him but I'm sure a proper upbringing and what amounts to an extended family of thousands of people all over the world will see him through. I can't wait to hop along for the ride.

When people speak of their work these days they frequently talk about 'putting out fires' and 'multi-tasking.' Technology has allowed individuals to jump from one project to another with amazing speed, to focus and refocus over and over again. Who hasn't wished to spend a month, a week, even a day for that matter, working on *just one thing?* Make it perfect. Make it right. No matter how long it takes or how inconvenient or unprofitable it is. 'Good enough' is never good enough when you are your own harshest critic. And, for me, that leads to the last piece of this coming-of-an-age story. The part about pure, unadulterated enthusiasm. You might call it naivete but we should all be so innocent that we would jump right into an endeavor we love without fear or second-thoughts and figure out the details as we go along.

I know the Scottish boy is like that, and just from looking at his big, curious eyes, I imagine the metal boy is too.

Jim Coudal
30th July 2003 Chicago

THE PROJECT

My interest in animation dates back to some of my earliest memories as a child. Like most young kids I loved watching cartoons on TV, and recall drawing pictures of my favourite animated characters at a very early age.

As I got a little older I became fascinated with the animation process itself and started making my own little flip-books. I also remember following instructions in a book on how to construct a zoetrope using card and paper clips. At the age of thirteen I bought a book based on the British TV series 'The Do-it-Yourself Film Animation Show,' and this more than anything else convinced me that it was possible to create my own animated films at home.

I got hold of an old Super-8 cine camera and prepared for my first attempt at home film-making. Initially I experimented with stop-motion animation using modelling-clay figures, mainly because it seemed like an easier option than drawing hundreds of individual pictures.

I constructed a little set using chopped up cardboard boxes with pillars made out of toilet roll tubes, and painted it to resemble stone. I sculpted a little character sitting on a stone throne with a dog-like creature sitting at his side. The only thing I remember about the film involved the character being revealed by the light of an opening door, as his servant marched in to greet him with a bow. There was no story or point to it whatsoever of course. None the less it was exciting to see something come to life on celluloid for the first time.

Feeling more adventurous I then built a crude rostrum set-up in the form of a wooden frame painted black with sidelights, baseboard and a hinged glass pressure plate.
I produced a couple of pencil tests, and even got as far as inking and painting a few animation cels, before getting side-tracked by my next master plan.

This appears to be the curse of most creative people - starting a project, only to abandon it at an early stage in favour of a 'better' idea that occurs to you along the way. One of my main

reasons for producing Rustboy was an attempt to put an end to this situation once and for all, making sure that I followed the project through to completion.

Being a big fan of Ray Harryhausen, the creative genius responsible for the stop-motion work in Jason and the Argonauts, the Sinbad movies, and many others, I started reading up on how to produce poseable rubber characters.
I learned how to construct metal armatures with crude ball and socket joints. In fact my dad would do most of the work on this part of the process (drilling holes in ball bearings isn't easy). I would then sculpt my character over the armature using modelling clay.
A plaster mould was produced from the sculpture, which could then be used to form a liquid-latex skin. This was fitted over the armature and filled with foam rubber chips to bulk it out. I really got into this at the time, and produced a number of models using this technique, but unfortunately didn't get round to doing very much animation with them.
As a little tribute to my earlier efforts, Rustboy's arms and legs were loosely based on the armatures I made for my stop-motion models back then.

And that was about the extent of my early attempts at animation as a teenager. It would take many years, and the advent of the home computer to get me back into it.

At the age of seventeen I spent two years at college studying basic graphic design. To be honest the course was quite poor, and didn't really teach me very much, but it *was* useful for building up a portfolio, which helped land my first job in the graphic design business working in a small studio.

I worked for various graphic design and advertising companies over the following years, gradually shifting from designer to illustrator in the process.

During this period I enjoyed working in a variety of mediums, using different styles of traditional illustration for brochures, corporate identity work, packaging, and advertising campaigns.

The greatest change to my working practice occurred when computers were introduced in the design industry, as they played an increasing role in my illustration work. But what excited me most was the possibility of using this new technology to get back into animation.

I bought my own Apple Mac computer and carried on with my illustration work for several years. By this time I had taken the plunge, and left my job to work freelance.

Since getting hooked on the computer, I had developed an interest in 3D, and played around with little animation tests whenever I had any spare time.

In fact I had been impressed and intrigued with 3D animation years before I ever laid hands on a computer, having seen films like the early Pixar shorts, Luxo Jr, Tin Toy, and Knick Knack, as well as the 3D sequences in Tron.

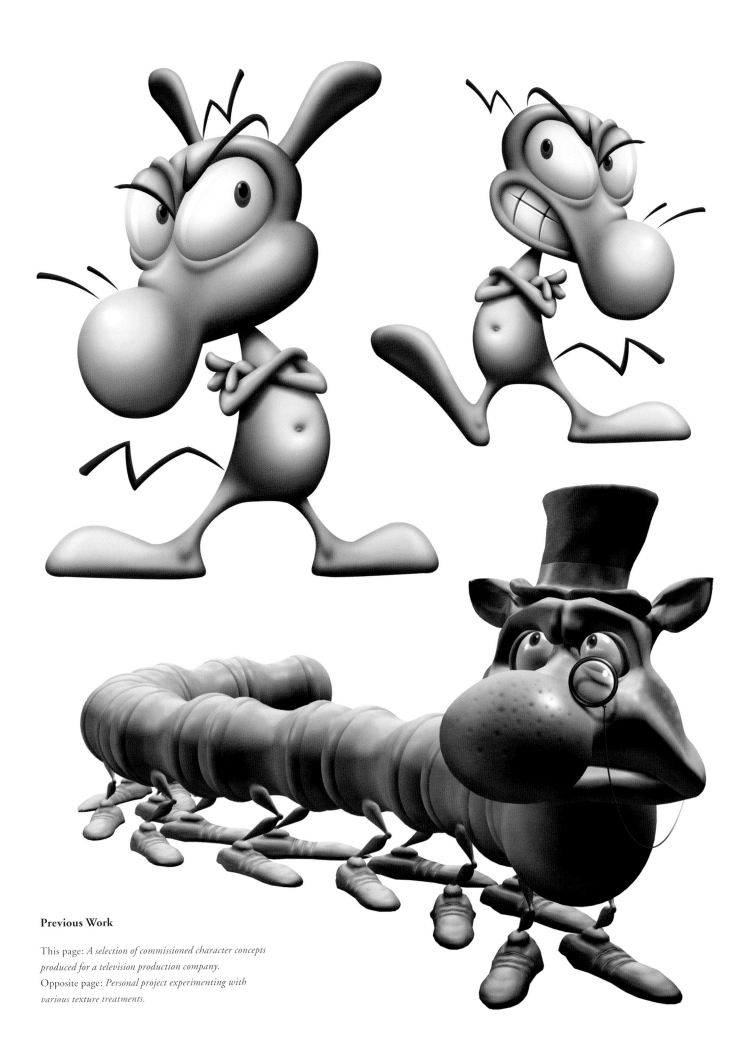

Previous Work

This page: *A selection of commissioned character concepts produced for a television production company.*
Opposite page: *Personal project experimenting with various texture treatments.*

By this time I had branched out a little from pure illustration to work in multimedia, game development, part-time teaching at art school, and concept work for a television production company. Some of these career moves didn't exactly work out the way I'd hoped, but I don't have any regrets. You learn from your mistakes.

One day I was thinking about all the projects I must have started over the years and never finished. I remembered how much I wanted to create a short film with my cine camera all those years ago, but was so frustrated with the results I was able to achieve with my limited equipment and facilities. I realised that I now

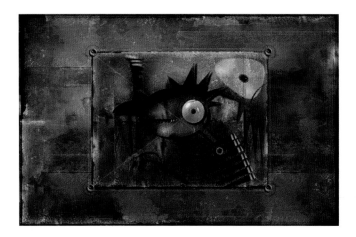

had everything I needed to produce a better film than I could ever have imagined back then, but was completely wasting the opportunity by doing nothing about it. Now was the time to make my short film. More importantly, I promised myself I'd finish it this time, however long it took to complete.

I was trying to think of a subject for my film when I found a small digital image of a character I'd created years earlier named Rustboy. I felt that the rusty character had potential as the star of my film, and set about thinking what could be done with him. The style of the picture suggested a cut-out animation technique, and I did consider this option for a while but decided that it would be too limiting. In the end I decided to redesign the character completely in 3D but retain the name.

After sketching out a few quick ideas of how he might look, I returned to the computer and started building him in 3D.

The next thing I needed was a story.

The basic idea of the story almost suggested itself through the look of the character. He seemed to have an inquisitive look on his face, mixed with a little sadness. I came up with the idea of Rustboy being accidentally brought to life during a lightning storm, much in the same way as Frankenstein's monster was born. I liked the idea of his being all alone, trying to discover who he was and where he came from. He starts off full of the joys of life, discovering new exciting things in this unfamiliar world he finds himself in, but slowly becomes bored, sad, and lonely when the reality of his situation sets in.

This was the rough starting point of the story that I would expand later, but it was enough to convince me that I was on the right track.

The first real piece of work I produced was the title sequence. It was a good way of establishing a feel for the project without going too far down the route of having to design anything specific. I wanted the titles to suggest some of the events that would occur later without being able to see them too clearly. This was achieved by keeping everything in the shadows and using pools of light to reveal hints of what was to come.

The title sequence was also useful for trying out a variety of techniques that I wanted to feature throughout the film.

All the shots used in the titles take place inside the mansion, and the only light source is moonlight shining through the windows. I wanted to show the effect of rain casting shadows on the main subject as it poured down the glass. I achieved this effect by creating an animated rain map using a variety of techniques, then applying this map to a spotlight as a gel. This produced the same effect as shining light through a film projector. I used this effect throughout most of the title sequence.

Another technique I tested was a simulated depth-of-field blur, achieved by rendering in layers. This was used primarily on the shot of the equipment that subsequently brings Rustboy to life. First of all I set up the entire shot with all the elements in place and the camera-move established. I made a duplicate of

The Starting Point

This page: *A selection of frames from the title sequence. This was the first piece of work produced for the Rustboy project.*
Opposite page: *This original Rustboy image was the inspiration for the redesigned 3D character.*

Title Sequence

*The titles were designed to set the
mood of the film by showing dimly
lit glimpses of what was to come.
The blue and sepia tints were
added in post production.*

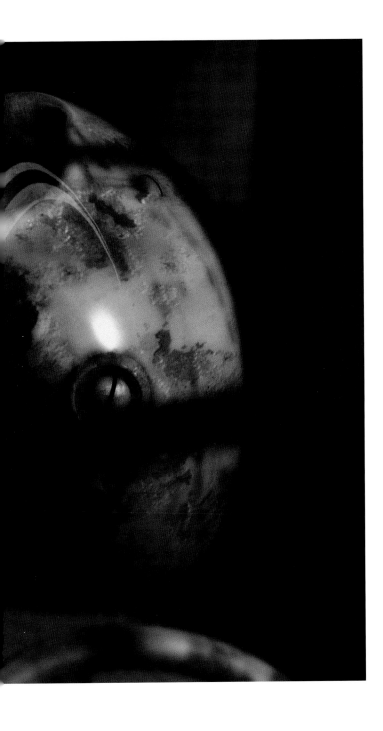

this work-file, deleting all the objects apart from those distant from the camera. I rendered this sequence of frames as the first pass. These frames were blurred using a 'Photoshop action,' then compiled into a movie-file. This would be my background layer. Next I returned to the original 3D work-file, this time deleting all the objects except those in the mid-distance. I imported my blurred background movie and set it as a background in the camera-view, then rendered the result as the next layer.

These frames were run through a 'Photoshop action' again, this time using a less pronounced blur, then compiled into a movie file. Finally the original work-file was opened once again, but now, only the foreground elements were used. The second blurred movie was imported as a background once again, and the sharp foreground objects rendered directly over the top.

This layering method can also be achieved by rendering the layers with 'alpha channels' and compositing them using software such as 'Adobe After Effects,' but the technique I've described above is the budget method.

One of the questions I'm asked most in relation to the title sequence, is how I created the water droplet. It was achieved using a simple lathed object. The object starts off as a shallow inverted dome and morphs over time into the full droplet shape. At the point where the drop appears to break, I added a sphere that matches the size and position of the bulbous portion of the drop. The sphere drops down out of frame while the droplet quickly morphs back to its original shape. The effect was completed with the addition of a second small sphere and a little wobble on the droplet at the end.

The original version of the title sequence featured temporary royalty-free music. This was replaced when I was approached by Erik Nickerson, who is now writing an original score for the film. Erik has worked on several musical ideas and themes for the film so far, and I am very pleased with the results.

Around the time I started out on the Rustboy project I was also considering trying to build my first website. This presented an opportunity to combine the two, as I thought it might be

A FILM BY BRIAN TAYLOR

RUSTBOY

BACKROOM FILMS PRESENTS AN XL5 PRODUCTION 'RUSTBOY'
WRITTEN, DESIGNED AND PRODUCED BY BRIAN TAYLOR

ENTER

THIS SITE REQUIRES FLASH 4 AND QUICKTIME 4

Rustboy Online

The Rustboy site was created to document the making of the film and generate interest in the project. The online presence has played a huge part in the success of the concept.

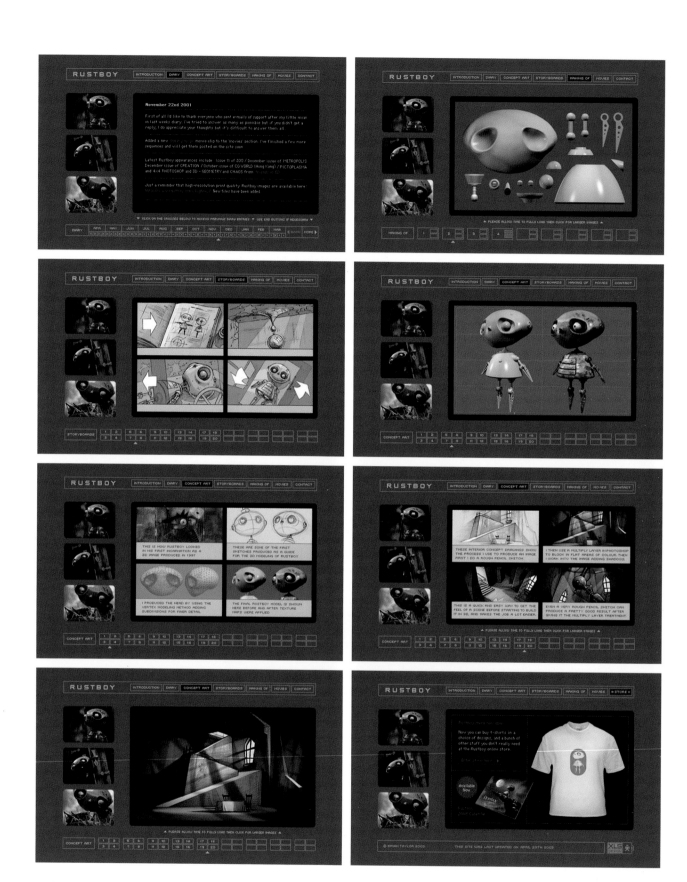

Rustboy Screenshots

*A selection of web screens showing the various
sections, including an ongoing production diary.*

interesting to create a site that documented the making of the film. I didn't know the first thing about web design but I'd done a little bit of animation using 'Macromedia Flash' and wondered if it would be feasible to use Flash to create the entire site, mainly to avoid having to learn how to use software I was unfamiliar with. It turned out to be fairly straightforward to produce, and worked just fine as a Flash site. Although I had no experience in web design, I did know one thing - nobody would visit the site if they didn't know it existed.

The night before I launched the website, I put together a list of around ten sites and a few magazines that I thought might be interested in helping spread the word. I sent them a small press-release style email announcing the launch of Rustboy.com.

I had no idea if this would have any effect whatsoever but I figured that there's no harm in trying.

I woke up next morning eager to check my email to see if anyone had replied, and I think it would be fair to say that the results were better than I could ever have imagined. The response was phenomenal with messages flooding in from people wishing me luck and offering support. Over the next few weeks the whole thing snowballed to the point where the site was receiving thousands of unique visitors each day.

Things got really weird when I started getting messages from industry professionals. One day it would be a couple of guys from Pixar, next it would be some of the people working on Lord of the Rings or Star Wars. It was very exciting and flattering on the one hand but a bit scary at the same time, knowing that I was being scrutinised by the people who make big blockbuster feature films. This really brought home to me how powerful the Internet can be.

My original plan for the short was a fairly modest production with an expected running time of around five minutes. When I started to appreciate the amount of interest the project was generating, it got me thinking - maybe I should set my sights a little higher. Rustboy had been featured in many books and magazines by this time and had even made the front cover of a few of them. Entertainment Weekly magazine included

me in the 2002 'It List' - the 100 most creative people in entertainment. It was becoming clear to me that this was outgrowing hobby status and could possibly be produced as a commercially viable product.

I was originally rendering the movie out at a relatively low resolution, thinking that it would be shown online at best, but when I started thinking bigger, I decided to re-render the work I'd done up to that point at broadcast quality. I also decided to expand the whole project in every way, and was now aiming at a running time of twenty-five minutes. I knew this was going to be a colossal amount of work for one person, but in a strange way it is the sheer scale and scope of the project that keeps me going. Most short films deliberately keep things simple, usually limiting the story to take place in one main setting. If I had set my film in one limited environment, I know that I would have become bored and given up by now. The diversity of the locations and the detail involved ensures that there is always a new challenge around the corner. As you can hopefully see from this book, Rustboy has been a lot of hard work so far, but I'm still enjoying every minute of it and I'm more committed than ever. I'm sure there are people out there who think I'm crazy for taking on a project of this size before cutting my teeth on something less adventurous, and they're probably right, but I've come this far and there's no turning back now.

On the subject of seeing the film through without getting sidetracked or put off by the daunting task ahead, I made a conscious decision not to enforce too much of a particular look. I like to work in different styles, which is fine most of the time for adding variety to the work I do, but it can also be a problem. I believe that this is one of the main reasons for abandoning personal projects in the past. I would be working on one project in a particular style, when I'd see something else that inspires me, in a completely different style. More often than not this

would give me cause to question what I was doing, resulting in quitting the current job in favour of starting something new, based on whatever I'd seen. With Rustboy I tried to start with a fairly neutral look, allowing the project to develop its own style as it progressed. I do feel that this is exactly what has happened, and I've found myself returning to some of the earlier work, changing it slightly to keep it in line with the overall style that has emerged.

I have had lots of influences and inspirations over the years including Ridley Scott (Alien, Blade Runner), Jean 'Moebius'

Giraud (French comic book artist), Ray Harryhausen (stop-motion animator), George Herriman (Krazy Kat comics), Chris Cunningham (video director), Vaughan Oliver (graphic designer), and Kyle Cooper (motion designer).

Inspirations for Rustboy specifically would include Paul Berry's 1991 short animation 'Sandman,' Tim Burton (The Nightmare Before Christmas), Jean-Pierre Jeunet (The City of Lost Children), early Disney animation (Snow White, Pinocchio), early horror movies (Frankenstein, Bride of Frankenstein) and German expressionist cinema (The Cabinet of Doctor Caligari).

Having decided to expand the scale of the project, my new plan was to produce the film as a DVD and possibly sell it to television networks for broadcast. I approached an individual with the prospect of looking at this as an investment opportunity, and soon found myself working on the project full-time.

During the production process so far, much has been written about Rustboy in magazines and online, some of which is not entirely true. Journalists have a tendency to be a little too creative with the facts, and I've had to cringe a few times reading stories of how I've supposedly turned down major job offers in Hollywood. Having said that, I have had quite a few genuine offers that I've declined or have been postponed for one reason or another. I was asked if I'd be interested in developing Rustboy as a feature film by the producer of a hit 2002 movie. I've been approached by more than one animation studio asking if I would consider taking a back seat as a creative consultant,

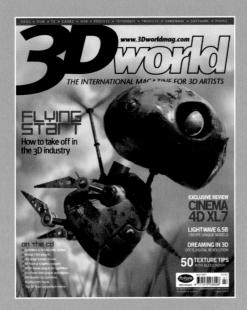

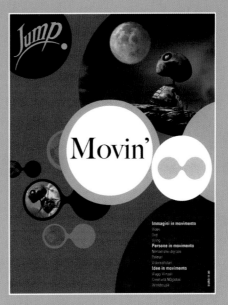

Storyboard Sketches

This page: *Storyboard panels for the title sequence, used to establish content and plan the various camera moves.*
Opposite page: *The first sketch of the redesigned 3D version of the character.*

allowing them to handle the production of the film. Other notes of interest have included everything from a Rustboy theme-park attraction to computer and console games.

Choosing to publicly document the making of the film from day one has had its pros and cons. On the positive side it has been a great way of generating publicity and general awareness well ahead of time, while building a potential future audience along the way. The downside is that there's a danger of some people feeling increasingly irritated by the amount of time the film is apparently taking to produce. Most animated films are in production for several years before the public knows anything about them. However, the pros far outweigh the cons, and the number of email messages of support I receive each day is a constant source of encouragement. I do occasionally hear people complaining that Rustboy is taking forever to complete, but I don't pay too much attention to them. It's important to me that this is done well, however long it takes.

Rustboy Montage

This image was produced for promotional purposes, and subsequently used on T-shirts, mouse-mats, and various other items to help fund the project.

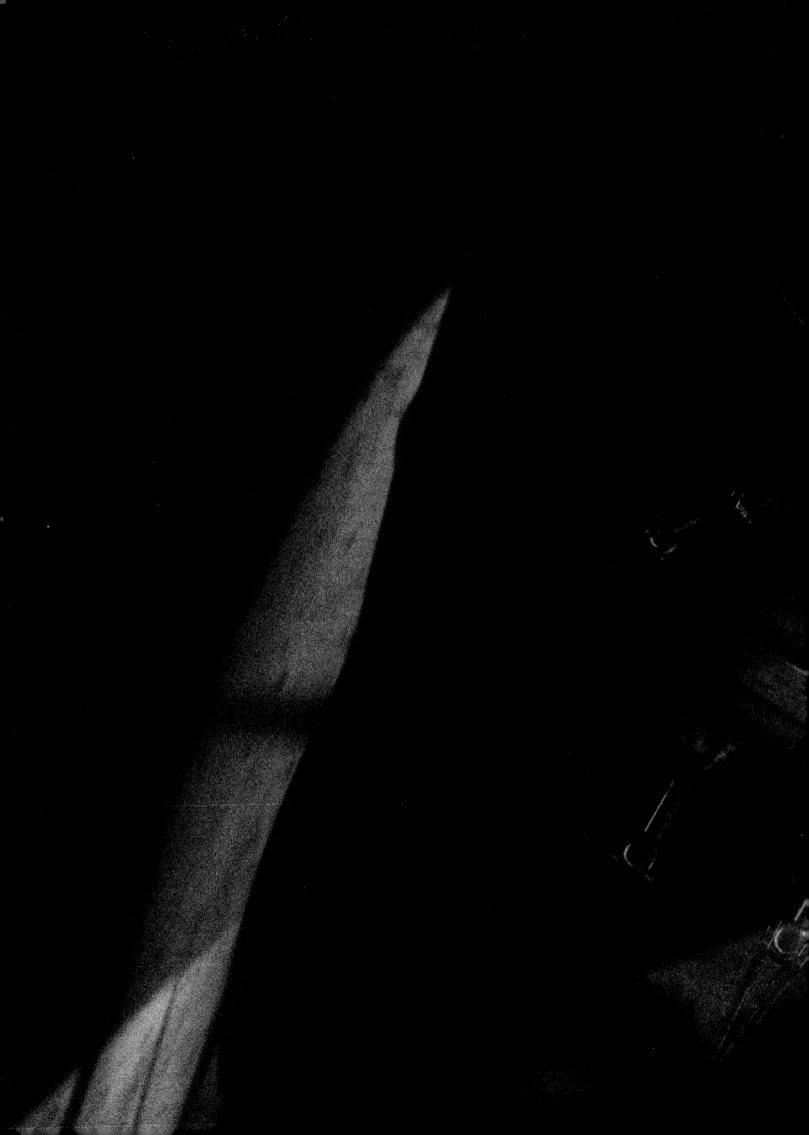

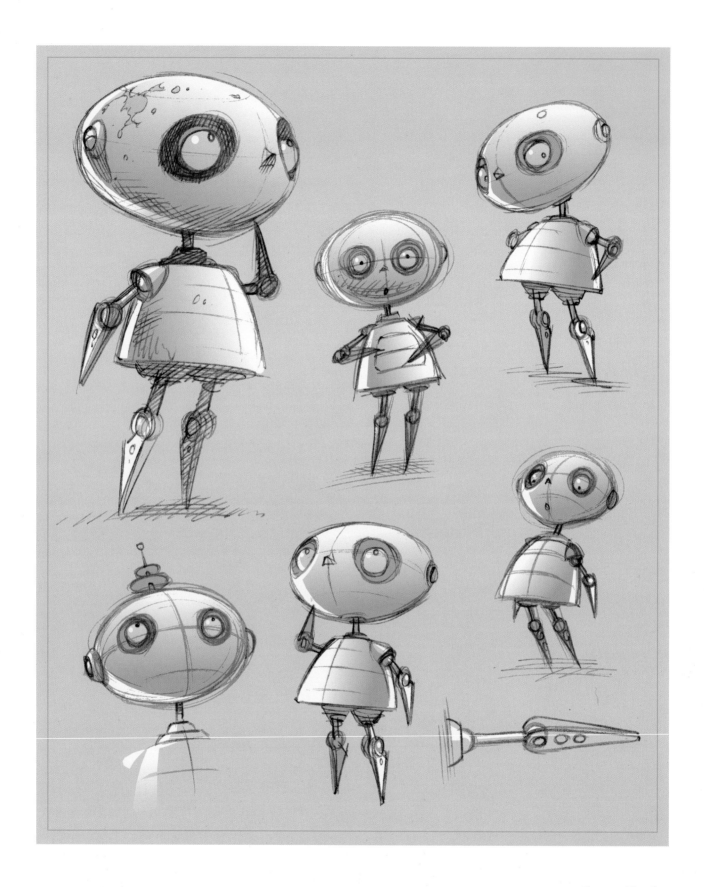

Concept Sketches

*A selection of concept designs produced to
establish the look of the character before
building the 3D model.*

THE CHARACTER

The first step in creating the 3D version of Rustboy was to sketch a few rough ideas on paper. I had the general look pretty much worked out in my head, and it didn't take many pencil drawings before I was happy enough to start building the character in three dimensions. I began by constructing his head using the vertex modelling method, starting with a default sphere, then adding and modifying points until I'd built the basic shape. When I was happy with the results I subdivided the model to smooth it off. The rest of the character was made up of simple lathed and extruded shapes. The whole design and modelling process was pretty straightforward, and the first attempt was the same Rustboy you see to this day with no modifications.

One of my intentions from the start, was an attempt to give the character a stop-motion feel. There's a certain look to many computer generated characters that doesn't particularly appeal to me, therefore I make a conscious effort to avoid that 'computery' look as much as possible. I received an email message of support from a colleague of the late Paul Berry whose short film 'Sandman' was an influence on Rustboy.

He told me that Paul, a stop-motion animator, wasn't a fan of computer generated films, but he reckons he would have liked this one. I was very flattered by the comment but also slightly spooked, as I had never mentioned the Sandman inspiration to anyone at the time.

Quite a number of people have brought up the subject of the film clips having a stop-motion quality. I even tried an animation test, attempting to emulate the jittery feel of stop-motion films at one point but it wasn't particularly successful.

The main rust texture for the character is one of the few photographic images used for my texture maps. I did modify the image quite a bit but I normally prefer to create my textures from scratch. Two texture layers are used for the character, one for the image and a corresponding greyscale version for specular and reflection maps. The panels on Rustboy's chest are images, and not part of the geometry of the body, simply because I couldn't figure out a way of modelling them successfully with

Hidden Talents

Rustboy discovers his flying capabilities. The propeller was a later modification to the character design, and an important part of the storyline.

my software of choice. I haven't had anyone comment about this, so I guess I've got away with it. I also used some artistic licence with the detail on the eye map. A small white specular highlight was added to the actual image of the iris, because the 'real' highlight didn't always register in certain lighting conditions. This made his eyes appear lifeless at times, and the addition of the little white dots ensure that they sparkle regardless of the lighting used.

All the textures were applied using cylindrical mapping or straight projection mapping. When I'm creating the texture for an object such as Rustboy's head, I use a grid technique to ensure that the image fits accurately around the model.
I start with a white background, and cover it with a large grid of, let's say, blue lines. I then colour every third or fourth line in red. When this texture template is wrapped around the head, it gives me a starting point to get my bearings.
I can see where the grid lines are positioned on the geometry, and use this to rough out basic coloured shapes on the texture to correspond with key areas of the model such as the eye sockets. After a little jumping back and forth between paint-program and 3D model, the resulting template can be used as a guide for the final texture map.

When the head texture was completed and applied, the next step was to fix the inevitable pinching effect at the top and bottom of the model caused by cylindrical mapping.
I added a new layer in the texture editor and imported a rust texture with an alpha mask creating a randomly shaped soft outline. This was applied as a straight map on top of the head, hiding the pinched area, with the soft edge blending into the main texture.

Building the 3D Character

Opposite page: *Rustboy is shown here before and after textures were applied. These are the main textures and environment map, although additional layers were required for reflection, specular, and bump mapping.*
This page: *The various components required to build the 3D character.*
Following pages: *Rustboy model sheets.*

The Rustboy storyline relies heavily on the character's ability to convey a broad range of emotions. At first he is frightened and confused by the strange surroundings he finds himself in. He has to convey curiosity, and the joy of discovering new and exciting things around every corner. As we progress through the film he feels sad and lonely, longing for a companion with whom to share his adventures. When the novelty of his limited world wears off, he slumps into depression and boredom.

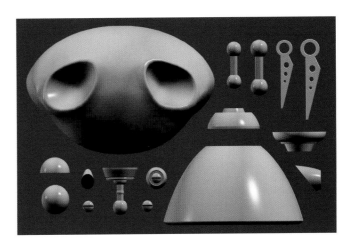

The difficulty arises when the ability to express these feelings is hampered by his lack of features and appendages. The simplicity of the character design and rigidity of his metallic exoskeleton don't exactly help when trying to convey fluid expressive movements. How does he scream, shout, laugh or smile when he doesn't have a mouth? How does he carry objects with no hands? How can he express anger with no eyebrows on that solid-state skull?

When I started thinking of the potential problems ahead due to these shortcomings, I experimented with a few modifications. I tried adding hands of every conceivable shape I could think of, but nothing worked at all. I attempted to redesign his arms altogether in order to accommodate the hands, but they all looked ridiculous. I went through the same process with different ideas for a mouth, but it changed the whole look of the character, so I decided to scrap it and leave him as he was. Rustboy's lack of detail and awkward proportions are part of his naive charm. I would have to figure out ways of working around the possible problems to preserve his appearance.

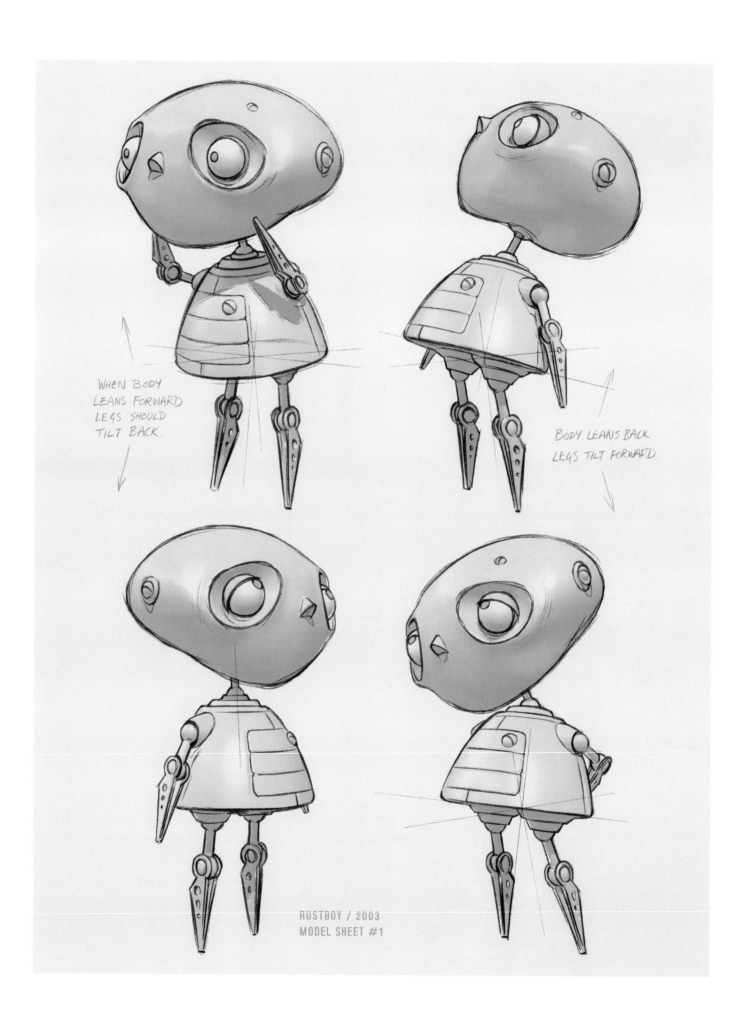

WHEN BODY
LEANS FORWARD
LEGS SHOULD
TILT BACK.

BODY LEANS BACK
LEGS TILT FORWARD

RUSTBOY / 2003
MODEL SHEET #1

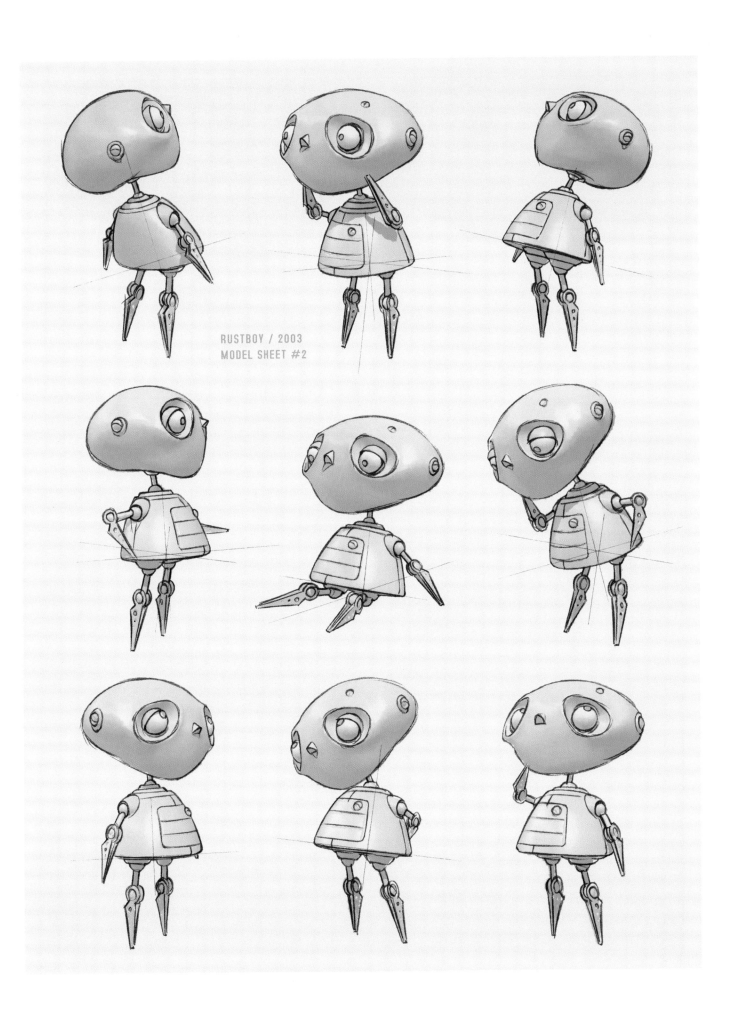

RUSTBOY / 2003
MODEL SHEET #2

As it happens, the absence of hands didn't turn out to be as big a problem as I had expected. I produced a test animation of Rustboy sneaking through the old mansion carrying a flaming torch. The torch was simply attached to Rustboy's arms and positioned to pivot at the tip where his hands should be, and it looked fine.

A greater worry was the length of his arms, or lack thereof. For example, a key scene required Rustboy to look through a telescope, but his arms were so short, that he couldn't reach anywhere near his eye.

The only way I could get around this was through the use of 'creative cropping.' I found that it looked okay if Rustboy started to lift up the telescope in long-shot, then I cut to a close-up of him continuing the movement up to his eye. In actual fact his arms are pulled a distance of around an arm and a half's length away from his body in the close-up shot. Because we only see his forearms and face in shot, there is no reference point to gauge what is happening around the shoulder area.

Getting back to Rustboy's head for a moment and the fact that he's somewhat facially challenged. The only moveable features available are his eyes and eyelids, which have to be used to convey a whole range of emotions. It's surprising how much feeling can be achieved through the eyes alone, but other elements will be required to truly capture the depth of emotion necessary.

Music will play a huge part in conveying the required feelings, and help the viewer empathise with Rustboy's innermost thoughts. Audiences tend to interpret imagery in their own way, but with the addition of music, you can almost force the viewer to feel what you want them to feel. The beauty of film music is that if done skilfully, it works on a subconscious level, affecting the viewer without them being aware of it. Of course music isn't only used to reinforce the character's emotion.

It can also be used to stir the audience's feelings from a voyeuristic viewpoint. For example, alerting the viewer to impending danger while the character is blissfully unaware. Music will be an important ingredient in the final Rustboy mix.

Another element that will help emphasise the emotional aspect of a particular scene in an even more subtle way, is the use of colour. I'll discuss later how colour shifts in the environment will be used to reinforce the changing mood of the character as the film progresses.

Mouth Tests

This page: *Various mouth tests were attempted, but abandoned to preserve the look of the character.*
Opposite page: *Rustboy discovers that rain is not good when you're made of metal.*

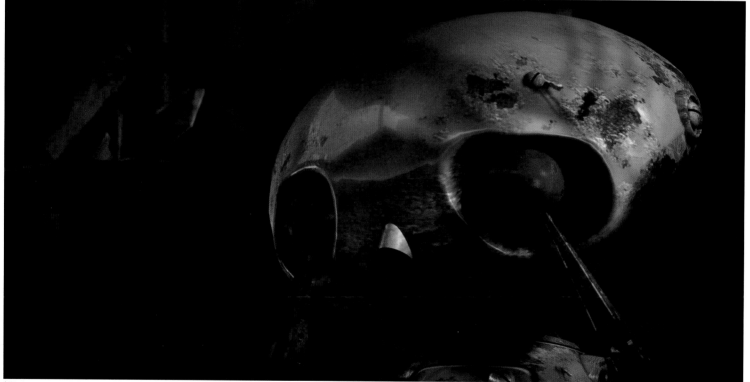

Creative Cropping

These images show how tight cropping was required to disguise the fact that the character's arms were too short to perform certain tasks.

As the popularity of Rustboy grew, I thought it would be interesting to see how he would translate into a plastic action figure. This was just a bit of fun at the time. I wasn't exactly serious about the idea, but I made up some virtual packaging and popped him inside. This reminded me of a process I'd read about for producing resin prototypes from virtual models.

I thought it would be useful to have a one-off Rustboy maquette made for storyboarding and promotional purposes, so I did a bit of online research to find out how much it would cost and if it would be feasible to produce. The process was stereolithography, and it wasn't long before I found a company with the necessary equipment to produce my Rustboy figure.

Stereolithography is a fabrication technology that produces solid physical models from 3D computer data. The process is used in many manufacturing industries for producing prototypes.
Due to its accuracy and surface finish, it has become the most popular of the rapid prototyping methods. It is a layered manufacturing method that utilises a photo-curable liquid resin in combination with an ultraviolet laser. A vat of the resin sits underneath the laser, and the laser 'draws' on the top layer of liquid. When the ultraviolet laser beam hits the liquid it hardens a small amount of resin under the beam point. By drawing the outline, then filling the outline of a layer, a solid layer of material is created. This layer is then lowered a small amount into the vat, a new layer of liquid is placed on top, and the process repeats itself. By creating one flat layer at a time, a very precise geometry can be created resulting in a complete part.

Eye Modification

The character originally had one eyelid, but a bottom lid was added later to help achieve subtle expressions. The single eyelid also looked strange when the eye was fully closed and viewed from the side.

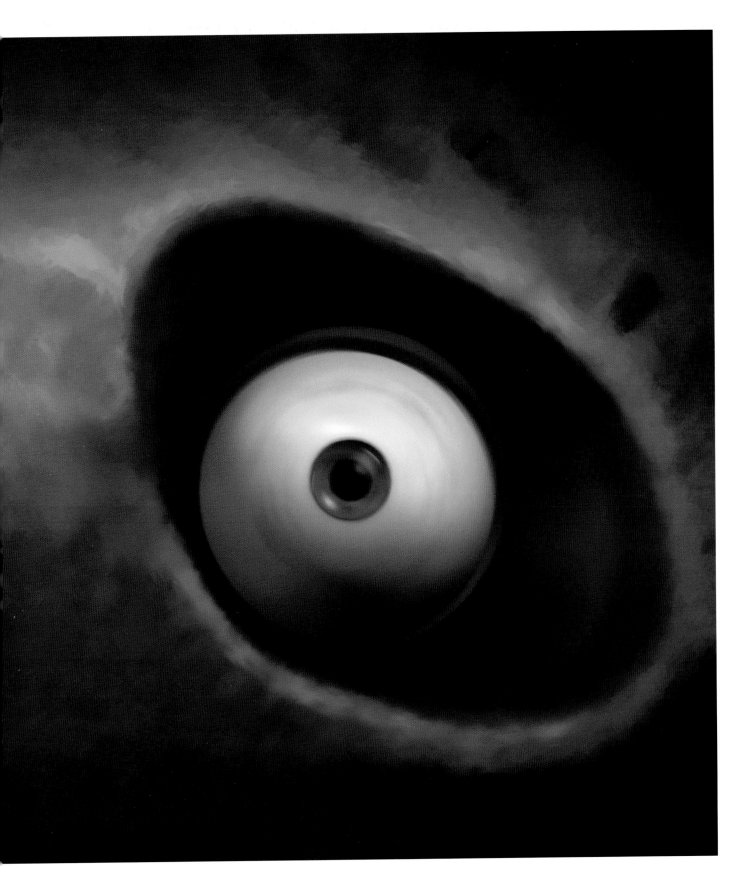

Illustrative Treatment

This style of illustration was produced for possible use in children's books and graphic novels.

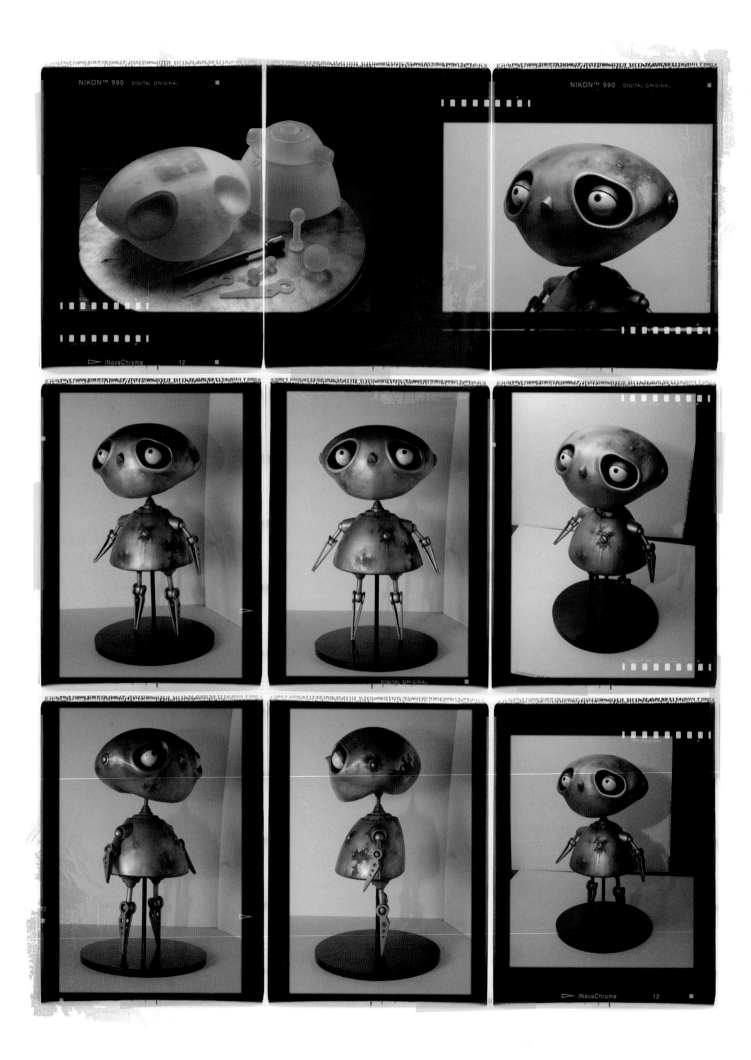

The maquette was made up of several of these parts. The head and body were both created in two pieces and fused together to form hollow shapes, to avoid excess weight. Separate pieces were produced for the arms, legs, neck and eyes.

I constructed the model, spray-painted him silver, and added the rust details. It was an odd feeling when the maquette was completed, and sitting on the table in front of me. The character that I knew so well in the virtual world I'd created for him was now a real tangible object, faithfully recreated down to every curve and detail.

Toys and Figures

*Opposite page: A physical prototype model
of the character was produced using
stereolithography.
The model was created in several parts,
then assembled and painted.
This page: A virtual action figure mock up.*

A few months later, back in the virtual realm, I worked on another version of a possible Rustboy toy. This time I was thinking about the 'designer' vinyl figure market, which is becoming increasingly popular. This was a chunkier version of the Rustboy model for practical manufacturing purposes. Coincidentally, just as I was fooling around with this idea, a toy company contacted me asking if I'd ever thought about producing a Rustboy figure.

I showed them the designs I'd been working on, and we discussed various possibilities for a while, but in the end they decided it would probably have to wait for their 2004 range of products due to manufacturing issues.

Some of the illustrations in this book go beyond the design for the film. I'm interested in how the character can be adapted for use in other areas by using different styles and treatments. Rustboy children's books have been suggested many times, and

the idea of graphic novels also interests me. Although Rustboy is being produced in 3D, I am a big fan of traditional Disney style cel animated movies, so I produced a 2D adaptation of the character just out of curiosity to see how flexible the design could be. Rustboy the cartoon series anybody? The images on pages 54-57 were originally produced for a Rustboy article and interview in a style/culture magazine in the UK. However, the

Vinyl Toy

Although this is a rendered mock up, a toy manufacturer has expressed interest in producing a vinyl Rustboy toy. This is a chunkier version of the model to aid the manufacturing process.

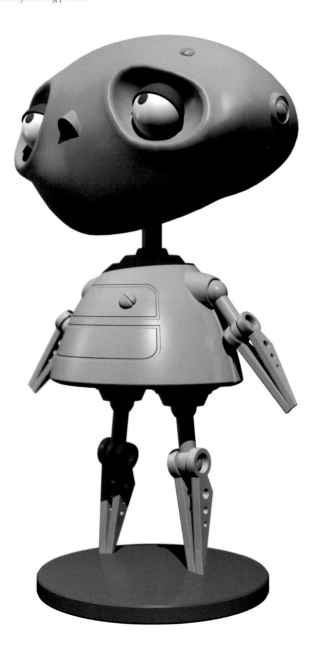

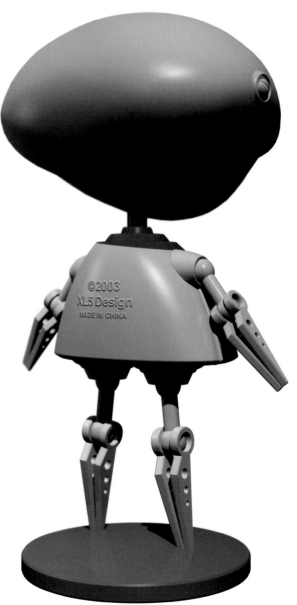

feature didn't go ahead as the journalist I was dealing with, landed a job with an American publication along the way. Judging by the email messages I receive, Rustboy has a wide appeal, and it is useful to have a portfolio of different treatments to suit various media requirements.

Returning to the film, one of the issues I had to determine was the height of the character in relation to his surroundings.
I figured that Rustboy stood at somewhere around two feet tall, but the mansion he had found himself occupying was that of his (human) creator. Now this made it easy enough to work out what size he *should* be, compared to the size of a room and the items within it. But I found that I had to cheat his scale in some cases just to make things *feel* right rather than be accurately proportioned.

A good example is the rowing boat Rustboy uses to set off on his ocean adventure. If he is seated in the boat at the correct scale, he looks ridiculously small.
I had to enlarge Rustboy considerably in order to make him feel right in comparison to the size of the boat. It is purely a case of composition and aesthetics with something like this. Rustboy and the boat need to look good as a whole, creating one overall shape that is pleasing to the eye.

This situation where aesthetics take precedence over realism, crops up in various aspects of making the film. I regularly use 'fake' lights to illuminate areas of interest when there is no possibility of an actual available light source, or disable the ability of certain objects to cast shadows, which obstruct important aspects of the scene. As long as something looks good, I have no qualms about breaking the rules in order to achieve the required result.

There *was* one small modification to the first Rustboy model that was added a little later. The story requires him to fly, so I later devised a hatch on his back that opens up to reveal a propeller. As the hatch opens, the folded rotor blades unfurl, then open like an umbrella ready for flight.

In one scene Rustboy is flying around puffy clouds in a dream sequence. The clouds were created using a modification of the multiplane technique developed in the early days of the Disney studios. The multiplane system uses a series of stacked glass plates on which different layers of artwork are placed. I used the same idea in 3D by mapping 2D cloud textures onto several layers of flat planes to create the impression of depth.

2D Variations

Opposite page: *These images were produced to test how the character might translate into a 2D cel animated film.*
This page: *Rustboy is given a traditional illustration treatment.*

Taking Flight

Having discovered that he can fly, Rustboy takes to the air for the first time after a shaky start. This image appeared on the cover of 3D World magazine, alongside a five-page Rustboy feature.

A cloud image was applied to each plane with a corresponding soft edged alpha-mask to produce a transparent background. The distant cloud planes were given an additional milky blue tint that increased in intensity the further they got from the camera for a feeling of atmosphere. This two dimensional plane technique produces quite a convincing effect of depth as the camera passes through the various layers of cloud.

Rustboy's recurring dreams usually revolve around two main subjects - his ability to fly, and the appearance of the mysterious Rustgirl. Is she the premonition of a future companion for Rustboy, or simply a figment of his imagination?

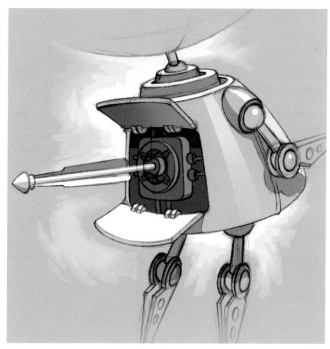

Flying High

Top: *Rustboy flies circles around puffy clouds
in one of his recurring dream sequences.*
Above: *Concept sketch showing the back
panel mechanism used to activate
the propeller blades.*
Following pages: *A series of four images
produced to accompany a style/culture
magazine feature.*

RUST boy

03448

03448

RUST boy

he saw a
faint glimmer
of light
far off in
the
distance

CHAPTER THREE

the MANSION

Mansion Concepts

The original mansion design featured a tall building that would later be modified for practical purposes.

THE MANSION

Much of the Rustboy story takes place in and around his creator's mansion. My first design featured a very tall, stylised house on top of a mountain, and much as I liked the look and feel of this version, it wasn't practical for several reasons.

The image looked good as a portrait shaped picture, but it just didn't work in the widescreen format I would be using for the film. It was impossible to frame the shot well as the subject either had to be miles away to fit it in, or there wouldn't be enough on show in close-ups.

The other problem with this over-stylised design was the fact that it was too steep a slope to incorporate the house entrance in the way I had intended.

The design I chose to go with was similar in style to the first, but vertically condensed to a manageable proportion. When it came to modelling the mansion on the computer, the original plan was to produce several different versions - one very simple model for distant views, a more detailed version for medium shots, and various sections of the mansion for extreme close-ups.

I began by blocking out the basic shapes of the simple version quickly in 3D. I wasn't attempting to copy my pencil sketch precisely with this model, but using it for inspiration while improvising along the way. In no time at all, the basic mansion was complete, with the addition of a few copied-and-pasted windows, and a hurriedly produced brick texture map.

The idea was that this would be a fairly quick mock-up to satisfy myself that the overall shape was working, then I'd go back and model it properly later. Instead I ended up adding details on top of this basic model, and never did get around to rebuilding the supposedly temporary parts.

In fact this grew into the main mansion model, with the addition of still finer details to withstand close scrutiny. I later reworked the texture map in more detail and the house was built.

Of all the stages involved in producing 3D work, modelling is without doubt my least favourite part of the process. I tend to work with very simple models and use textures and lighting

The Mansion Takes Shape

The second mansion design was more or less followed through to the final 3D model.

to add detail. I probably spend more time getting the lighting right, than everything else put together. But more on that later.

Although CG and digital film-making is a relatively new and hi-tech medium, I often employ age-old techniques borrowed from live action movies in my compositing work. Rustboy's opening shot of the slow approach to the mansion utilises a few examples of this. The first is the use of travelling mattes. Filming an actor against a blue-screen is a technique used to extract a matte, which can then be used to incorporate the footage of the actor against a new background. A Google search will deliver a wealth of information on this subject. I produced a travelling matte for the opening sequence, to incorporate various effects, including completely replacing the sky behind the mansion at a later date without having to re-render the whole scene.

The matte was simply created by returning to the opening sequence work-file and deleting the sky dome and all the lights. The scene was rendered against white to produce a black silhouette of all the elements in front of the sky. The resulting footage is your travelling matte, which corresponds to the original camera move.

This matte or mask can then be used within your compositing software to drop new elements behind objects in your original rendered footage. I use this method regularly to make various alterations to rendered footage after the fact.

Another technique I use often is a simple double-exposure - an effect that dates back to the dawn of film-making itself. This was used in the opening shot to add the moon and incorporate the ocean waves crashing against the side of the mansion.

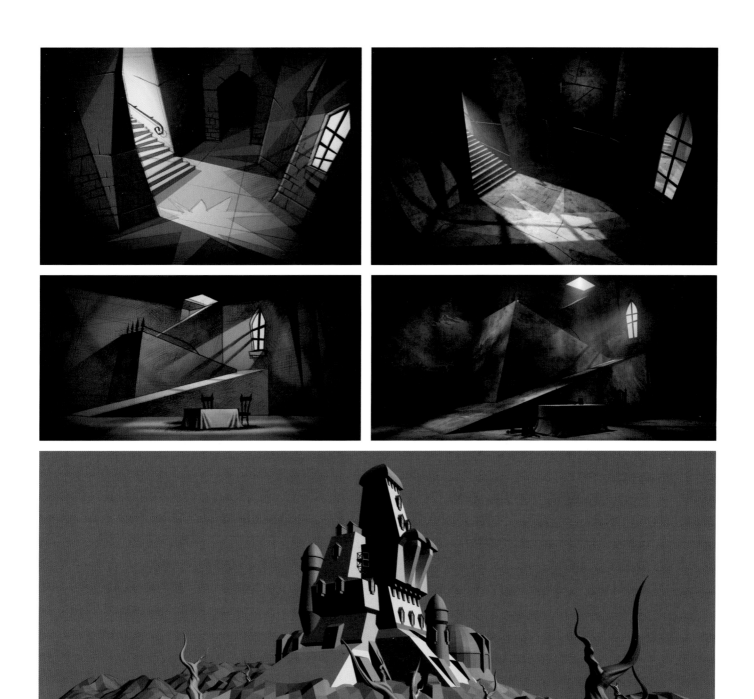

Concept Comparisons

*Top: These interior concepts show the
transition from the original designs through
to the final rendered scenes.*
*Above: The opening shot is shown here before
the final lighting and textures were applied.*

Opening Sequence

*The final rendered mansion exterior as it
appears in the film's establishing shot.*

The waves were produced by mapping real film-footage on a flat plane and positioning it in the appropriate place within the opening scene. The plane was self-illuminated and all the lights were deleted from the scene once again. This resulted in a completely black frame with only the waves showing, and any objects passing in front of the plane would also appear in black. This clip was rendered out and composited with the original opening sequence using the 'screen' blending mode.

Main Entrance

The original entrance concept sketch and the final 3D model seen here with early morning lighting.

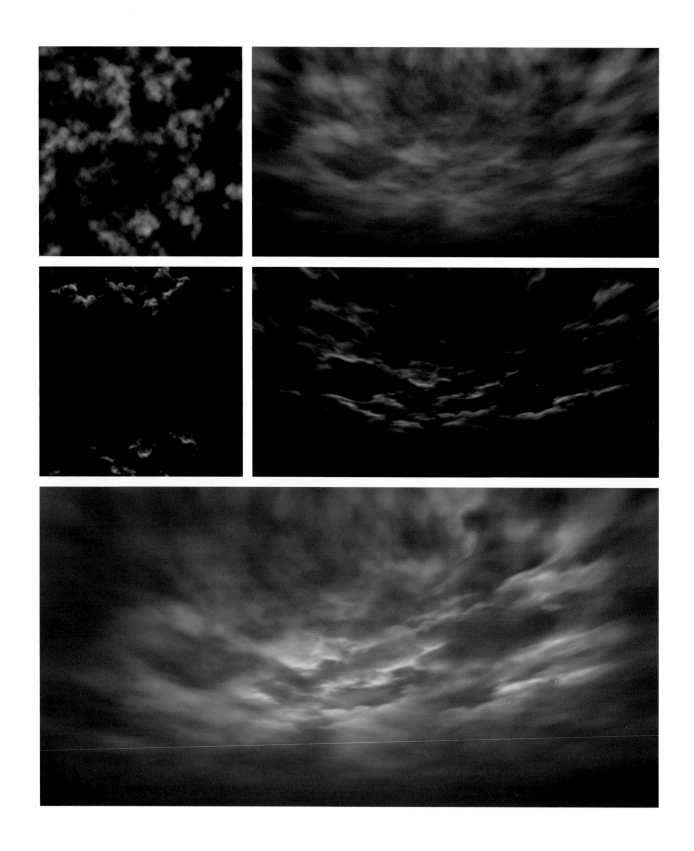

Layered Clouds

This series of images shows two cloud textures before and after they've been applied to a dome. The main image shows the final sky produced by combining the resulting footage using the 'screen' mode.

I created the sky in the opening sequence using the well known sky-dome technique, but I like to do it with a difference.

When creating a sky-dome, a large texture map with 'polar distortion' is normally used to compensate for the distortion caused by the dome shape. In most cases I prefer to utilise this distortion to dramatic effect, as shown in the example opposite.

From a composition point of view I like the cloud shapes created by wrapping the image around a dome, as they help draw your eye to the central focus of attention. I use two domes for my skies, one slightly larger than the other, with a custom made tiled cloud map applied. The black areas around the clouds are made transparent on the inner dome, to show another layer of clouds on the outer one. Both domes are rotated slowly to produce the effect of cloud movement, with the inner dome moving slightly faster, resulting in a more interesting blending effect.

For this particular example I took it to another stage, adding a little more depth, and including rim lighting from the moon. I repeated the process above, replacing the texture map with a corresponding image showing only the rims of the clouds. Both of these stages were rendered out to produce two clips of moving

Cloud Composite

A dramatic low-angle view of the mansion with the cloudy sky described opposite, and two early sketches of Rustboy exploring the rooms.

cloud footage. I altered the cloud rim clip by compositing a soft edged black mask in 'multiply' mode, blacking out much of the cloud, leaving only an area in the centre-right of the frame.
This clip was then composited with the original cloud footage in 'screen' mode to produce the final effect. The result was a cloudy sky moving realistically, with the edges of the cloud illuminated only within the moonlit area.

So let's take a guided tour of the mansion, starting with the main entrance. I always had a pretty fixed idea in my mind of how the entrance should look, and the metamorphosis from pencil sketch to final 3D model remained faithful to that vision.
This is a good example of my background in illustration influencing the way I handled the finished scene. If you look at the stonework around the front door, you will notice that it isn't constant across the entire wall. The stone bricks are

The Entrance Hall

This page: Four views of the grand stairway as you enter the hall. This is the space immediately inside the main entrance.
Opposite page: A painterly shot of Rustboy exploring the mansion.

very pronounced and three dimensional around the doorway, but they gradually fade to a subtle hint of brickwork at the outermost area of the frame. This is done to centre the focus of attention on the subject, a technique commonly used in drawing and painting.

I tried to give the overall look of the entrance a painterly feel, in the style of the painted background plates used in classic Disney features. In fact the whole mansion is an eclectic mix of styles and influences - Gothic, German expressionist, 30's retro, 50's retro, fairy tale kitsch, it's all in there somewhere.
Moving up the steps past the stone gargoyles, one of several recurring themes throughout the mansion, we enter the hall.

The stairway in the hall is the main access to all the other areas inside the mansion. At one stage I was thinking of planning out the layout of all the rooms in the house accurately, like an architectural drawing, but I decided this was not necessary. There are now several key areas in the mansion linked by various incidental corridors and passageways.
This allows for greater flexibility when planning how one shot or scene leads into the next. Many of these intermediate areas of the mansion will be built as I go along to accommodate the

Rustboy's Creator

*This page: The skeletal remains of
Rustboy's creator lie crumbling in the
dust and rubble of the mansion.
Opposite page: Rustboy is dwarfed by the
grand stairway in the entrance hall.*

requirements of a particular shot. In the process of creating the key areas, I've built up a library of architectural features and props that can be combined in various ways to quickly assemble these spaces. The shot of Rustboy sneaking around with the torch is an example of this mix-and-match approach.

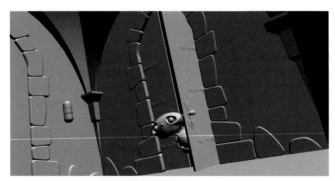

Next is the attic tower leading down to the laboratory area - this is Rustboy's birthplace, an unapologetic homage to the 30's Universal Frankenstein movies starring Boris Karloff. I loved those films as a kid, and have fond memories of our babysitter allowing my sister and me to stay up late to watch them on TV. I often describe Rustboy as a cross between Frankenstein and Pinocchio, and there are several references to both in the film, including a few of them in this book.

During the start of the film, the mansion is being battered by a raging thunderstorm. This isn't the first storm it has seen, but it's the worst. An almighty crash of thunder is followed by a flash of lightning that splits the roof of the attic tower revealing a large metal globe. A second lightning flash brings the globe to life and sends sparks of electricity down a succession of machines

Lighting a Scene

Top: Rustboy sneaks warily along a dark passageway illuminated by the light of a torch. Left: This shot demonstrated how a relatively simple scene is transformed with the addition of texture and dramatic lighting.

Lightning Sequence

*These storyboard panels show the sequence
of events leading up to Rustboy's birth scene.
The images were produced before
the laboratory was fully designed.*

was to use a monotone-blue colour from the opening sequence right through to the point after Rustboy is brought to life.

After some consideration I decided to introduce a secondary orange colour at the point after the lightning strikes for the second time. This would be used to subtly inform the viewer that a change of events was about to occur - a subconscious forewarning of the impending birth scene.

Having decided on the final laboratory design in sketch form, I took it to the next stage, a full colour concept illustration.

This is the method I normally use to create my final stage concept work. I start off with a tidied up pencil drawing that is scanned into the computer. The resulting image is placed on the top layer in Photoshop and set to 'multiply' mode. Two or three additional layers are added below the drawing, each used to differentiate between the various elements in the scene.

Working within these layers I draw selections around areas of the drawing and fill them in with flat colours until the

in a chain reaction. In the laboratory below, dials and gauges light up, and their pointers spin furiously into action. Electricity courses down through the wires and machinery until it reaches a device above Rustboy and discharges all its energy into him. Our hero is alive.

Unlike Rustboy and the mansion exterior, the laboratory went through several design changes and ideas before arriving at something I was happy with. This is the setting for the first key scene in the film therefore it's an important one.

I always knew it was going to have that 30's Frankenstein-set look, and it took a number of variations before I got it right, but the main change concerned the colour scheme. My original idea

Lightning Strike

Opposite page: *The final shot of the lightning splitting the roof of the attic tower was achieved using a variety of effects including particles and a custom created smoke texture movie.*
This page: *Concept sketches of the observatory adjoining the mansion, and an early entrance hall design in various colour studies.*

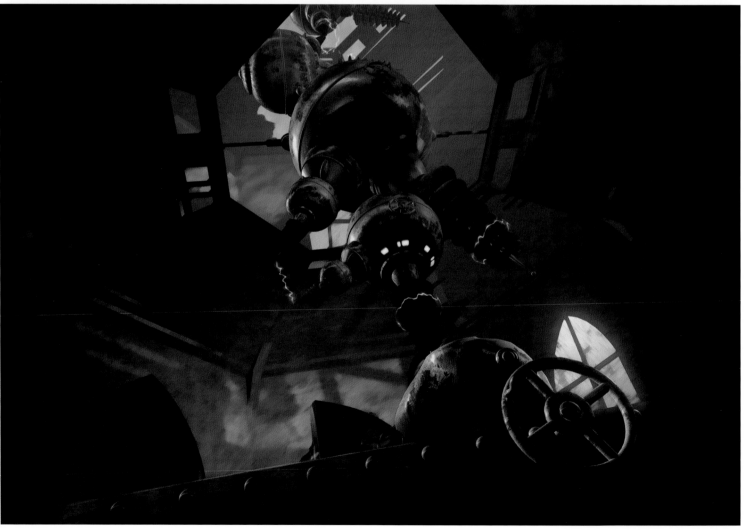

picture is fully built up. I then work into each layer adding shadows, highlights, and selective soft edged dark areas using large feathered selections. For the laboratory illustration, an additional layer was added between the background and foreground elements to produce the orange glow. This layer was completely filled with black, the glow added, and the layer set to 'screen' mode.

The final 3D laboratory scene was perhaps the most faithful to the original concept art, both in terms of content and colour. This demonstrates how useful the concept stage can be, in determining the layout, mood, and colour scheme fairly quickly and easily before venturing into the 3D process.

For example, I doubt that the idea of adding the orange glow in the background would have occurred to me, had I jumped straight into building the scene in three dimensions.

The Laboratory

Opposite page: *The machinery in the attic tower leading down to an earlier version of the laboratory setting.*
This page: *Various concept drawings of the laboratory where Rustboy is accidentally brought to life.*

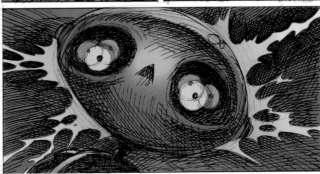

Laboratory Progression

These images show two stages of the final laboratory concept illustration followed by the finished 3D scene. Note how the final result is faithful to the concept in almost every detail in this particular case.

This helps give the laboratory an almost illustrative quality rather than being too literal or realistic with the lighting.

The next key area of the mansion is the study. This is one of the most widely used rooms in the film, and the main setting for Rustboy's quest to discover his reason for being.

I chose a predominantly golden-brown colour scheme for the study to suggest a musty sense of the past, and a source of forgotten treasures. The images here show only the basic details and furnishings. Specific props that require the character's interaction will be added to the study later.

This is where Rustboy first encounters strange unfamiliar objects that we take for granted. He doesn't understand the purpose of anything. This provides an opportunity to throw in a few visual gags to help the viewer warm to the character.

The lighting used in the study is typical of most of my 3D work. I generally use spotlights to illuminate a scene with soft pools of light, often assigning masks to the lights using soft edged random patterns to cast subtle fake shadows across a scene.

This is another technique borrowed from live-action cinema and theatre work, where a scrim is used to diffuse the light.

Rustboy's First Day

Above: *Concept sketch of the window shutters opening to reveal the morning light of Rustboy's first day.*
Below: *This shot of the character looking through a magnifying glass was staged against a backdrop to save rendering excessive background geometry.*
Opposite page: *Rustboy tries to figure a way out of the mansion to explore his new world.*

The Study

This is the setting for many of the indoor shots and a place of discovery for Rustboy. Each scene in the film requires at least two different lighting conditions for day and night.

A scrim is a translucent material such as gauze, usually covered with a random pattern to produce a dappled effect when placed in front of a light source.

In addition to lighting I often add fog to my scenes to create a feeling of atmosphere. Sometimes the fog effect is subtle, other times more pronounced, either way it gives a scene a greater sense of depth and scale by toning down distant objects.
This effect is known as 'ariel perspective,' another technique widely used in painting.

The study setting was used to test the idea of using a simple backdrop in certain close-up shots to avoid unnecessary rendering of the background geometry. The shot where Rustboy looks through a magnifying glass utilises this technique with a pre-rendered and blurred image of the study mapped onto a slightly curved backdrop within the scene.
This not only avoids the excessive geometry of the room, but also provides a built in depth-of-field effect with dramatically improved rendering times. To add a finishing touch, two

glowing lights were positioned to match the windows on the backdrop image. This glow would spill light over the foreground elements to help sell the idea.

Each of the interior environments requires two different lighting set-ups to represent day and night. In addition to this, the mansion entrance also has a snow covered winter variation. I decided to add a winter section to the longer version of the film for several reasons. It helps imply that the story spans a reasonable period of time, whilst adding visual interest and variation to the film in general. However the main reason

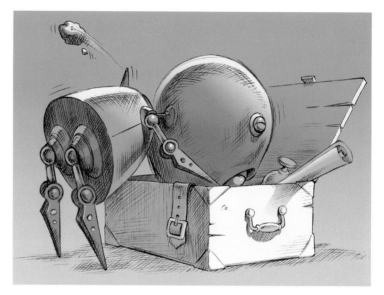
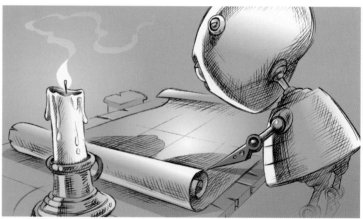

The Study in Detail

Opposite page: *Various views of the study and
a selection of concept sketches showing Rustboy
rummaging around for information
regarding his origins.*
This page: *A few of the details inside the study.*

Winter Setting

*Later in the film several locations require a
snowy winter variation. This was used in
part to help emphasise the character's mental
decline and escalating feeling of solitude.*

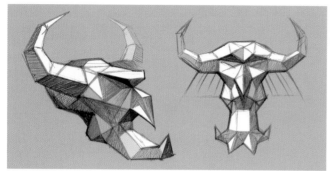

was to emphasise Rustboy's emotional decline. His feelings of depression, boredom, and loneliness will be heightened as he trudges through the snow in bleak blizzard conditions.

This idea was partly inspired by the classic 1941 'Tom and Jerry' cartoon, 'The Night Before Christmas.' You can't help but feel sorry for the little mouse locked out in the snow by the increasingly guilt-ridden Tom. It's a case of using the environment to help reinforce the emotional state of the character.

Underneath the mansion is the crypt – a series of adjoining chambers suspended by large stone pillars. I produced several pillar designs for use throughout the mansion, although the most frequently used was the version featuring the recurring gargoyle theme. A bump map was used to give the impression of chips on the stonework. You will notice that this detail is widely used on many of the props in the film.

During the latter half of the film, Rustboy has a series of dream sequences. Most of these dreams occur while he's asleep but I also built a drawing room set with a large fireplace to facilitate a daydream sequence while he sits gazing into the flames.

The fireplace features a pair of carved demonic stone heads. These sculptures were built as simple vertex models with no smoothing, creating a sharp angular look similar to the crouching gargoyles.

This scene is another example of using the whole picture as a metaphor for Rustboy's frame of mind at a particular point in time. I was trying to convey feelings of solitude, insignificance, helplessness, and a longing for something bigger and better. There must be more to life than this.

Building the Fireplace

Starting off with a few pencil sketches, a demonic stone sculpture was created as a vertex model with smoothing turned off to produce sharp edges. The main fireplace was built and textured, with bump maps used for the chipped stone effect and decoration around the iron hood.

The Drawing Room

Mesmerised by the dancing flames, Rustboy
drifts into one of his daydreams.
The fireplace model as it appears in the
finished drawing room setting.

Pillar Designs

This page: *Pillars are featured in several areas throughout the mansion including the underground crypt shown above.*
Opposite page: *Rustboy promotional poster.*

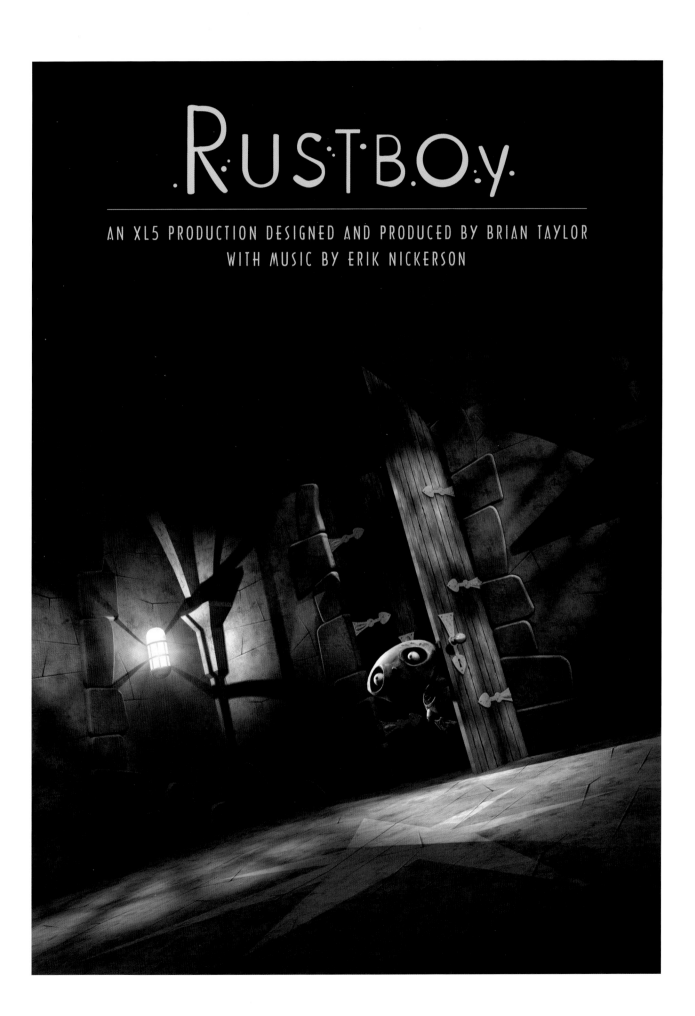

RUSTBOY

AN XL5 PRODUCTION DESIGNED AND PRODUCED BY BRIAN TAYLOR
WITH MUSIC BY ERIK NICKERSON

CHAPTER FOUR

the ISLAND

Leaving the House

*This concept picture is a combination of
rendered image and digitally painted
foreground mountains to quickly establish a
feel for the area beyond the mansion.*

THE ISLAND

The mansion in the story is situated on an uninhabited island to establish Rustboy's isolation and confinement. The difficulty with the design of the island was that it had to look interesting enough to hold the viewers attention whilst being relatively featureless in order to drive Rustboy to boredom.

I wanted the island to have a slight fantasy look without suggesting that it were set in another world. Arguably the secret of making a story like this work, is not to specify the time or place, allowing the viewer to let their own imagination fill in the blanks.

I was concerned that the outdoor environments might look like they had been created using an existing landscape generation program. I go out of my way to put my own stamp on any work I produce digitally avoiding 'the look' of the particular software I'm using. This is generally a case of coming up with my own methods of achieving as much as possible without accepting the built-in capabilities of the software.

As I'm standing next to my soapbox I might as well get right up there and voice my concern over the way a lot of software seems to be going these days. Everywhere you turn there are new features or plug-ins to do every conceivable part of the job for you. Now I'm sure some would argue that this helps speed up workflow, but there is a danger that these 'improvements' are turning the creative process into the digital equivalent of 'painting by numbers.'

The landscape immediately surrounding the mansion is a bleak rocky place and I felt that some visual interest was required as Rustboy sets off on the first journey beyond his home.
I drew up some concepts of the next area, filled with various rock formations. The first of these images was a view looking back towards the mansion, using a rendered background with digitally painted rocks in front.
This was a quick way of getting the look and feel correct before starting any 3D work. I liked the direction this mountainous region was heading and sketched a few more concepts of the

general area. Once I was satisfied with the overall look of this landscape setting, I began to construct a selection of rock formations based on the line drawings I'd produced.

Within the vertex modeller I began with simple default spheres, selecting points and dragging them around to establish the basic rock shapes. At this stage I would normally subdivide the geometry, adding detail and complexity to the model.

Rock Formations

These two pages feature a selection of concept illustrations, colour studies, and first stage 3D renders of the rocky landscape surrounding the mansion.

As it turned out, the simple first stage low-resolution models produced the exact look I had envisaged. This was achieved by experimenting with the smoothing-angle settings until I was happy with the mix of soft shapes and sharp creased edges.
I built a selection of these rocks and arranged them in various shapes and sizes to form my mountain clusters.

The concept illustration featuring the large boulder leaning over to form a short tunnel is shown here in three different colour variations. The following technique is one I often use to quickly test out various colour schemes.
The image was built up using the same method mentioned earlier, but the colour for each light source was applied on separate layers. This makes it easy to use the colour balance

Creating a Tree

The top image is the result of using shallow discs to form the foliage of a tree swaying in the breeze. Each disc is mapped with an animated cluster of leaves, with a corresponding alpha-mask used to render the black background portions invisible. The discs are also gently animated in a swaying motion.

sliders to try various possible colour combinations including day and night. The main image shows the final colour scheme I eventually decided on for the rocky mountain scenes.

I wanted Rustboy to feel frightened and wary as he wanders cautiously through these ominous monolithic structures on his first journey away from home.

As he travels beyond the mountainous region, the landscape gradually opens out into greener pastures with small rocky outcrops leading to a group of trees. After the static foreboding nature of the previous scene, I wanted this setting to feel alive and friendly in comparison, making Rustboy feel that he was now in a safe place.

The following technique was used to create trees with their leaves swaying in the breeze. I began by modelling a few leaves and arranging them in a bunch against a black background. The leaves were animated in a slight shimmering motion and rendered as a loop with an alpha-mask. The mask is used to give the impression that the leaves are cut out, with the black background appearing invisible.

This animated loop was mapped on to saucer-shaped discs that were arranged around the top of the tree trunk to form the

Landscape Concepts

*A series of concept sketches and colour studies including
the transition from rocky ground to grassland.*

greenery, and animated to sway gently. The combination of the swaying discs and animated leaves produce quite a convincing tree gently blowing in the breeze.

It's worth pointing out at this stage that the daylight scenes will always appear to take place in perpetual dawn or dusk.
I felt that this was important to keep the dark Gothic feel throughout the film, as setting scenes in broad daylight would be too great a contrast to the darker side of the story.

The tale reaches another key stage in and around this grassy setting when Rustboy happens upon a cricket sitting on a mound of earth. At first this is just another random object he knows nothing about, but this one is different.
When he tentatively prods it, out of curiosity, the cricket leaps in the air causing Rustboy to jump out of his skin. This is the first living thing he has encountered. Once he has recovered from the shock, he starts chasing his new friend through the grass, leaping with excitement in an attempt to mimic the insect.

My original designs for the cricket were stylised caricatures. However, this would imply that the cricket was a character, whilst it was important to the story that the insect be perceived as an ordinary creature.
For this reason I decided to go with a realistic version. Although the cricket is just an ordinary insect from the audience's point of view, it means a lot to Rustboy on various levels and eventually leads him to find a vital clue to his ongoing personal quest.

The partnership of Rustboy and the cricket seems to be a successful one that somehow strikes a chord with many people. The image of the character looking inquisitively at the insect is by far the most widely used picture in magazine and web articles. In the original short version of the story, the cricket only made a small appearance, but now that the film has been expanded, it is more fully integrated into the story.

Rustboy plays around with the cricket for a while and it eventually leaps onto a stone in a small pond. He skids to a halt

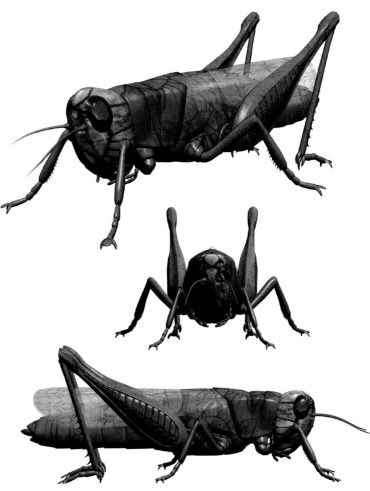

Rustboy and the Cricket

*Opposite page: Rustboy looks curiously at the first living thing he has encountered on the island.
This page: The partial wireframe render above reveals the geometry involved in the scene shown opposite. Three cricket studies displayed from various angles.*

The Boy in the Pond

*Chasing the cricket accidentally leads Rustboy
to discover his reflection in a small pond.*

at the edge of the water, almost instinctively knowing not to
venture any further. Kneeling at the side of the pond to see if
he can reach the insect, something else catches his attention.
He looks into the water, and sees his own reflection for the first
time. This significant sighting ties in with something he had
discovered in the study during his earlier detective work and
sparks off the next chain of events.

The pond setting shows how I've tried to suggest a fantasy feel
with otherwise ordinary elements such as the uprooted tree
stump. The gnarled roots of the tree create some interesting
shapes to help frame the shot. In hindsight I may add some
more trees or bushes in the background to enclose the setting
a little more.

Grassy Fields

A particle system was used to generate grass. By altering the characteristics of the particle emitters, the grass length, density, and patchiness could be controlled.

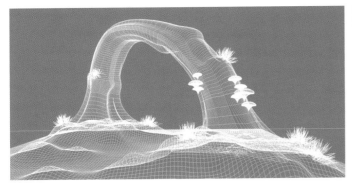

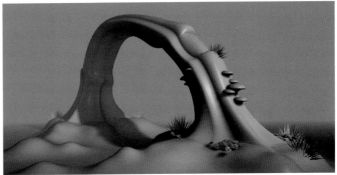

One of the images I had in mind for this section was Rustboy chasing the cricket through grassy fields. I achieved the grass by using a particle system. I set the particles to emit over a large area and specified that they freeze after one frame.

The particles were set to render as polygonal planes and to always face the camera. An image of grass blades was then mapped to the planes and an alpha-mask used to render the background transparent. I created three or four different grass maps for variation, to help avoid seeing repeating textures.

This grass technique looks very effective during slow camera moves, showing the three dimensional quality of each blade. After some experimentation I found that blurring the grass textures and alpha-masks produced a great depth-of-field effect. Because the blurring is relative to the viewing distance, the far away grass looks in focus, while the close-up blades are blurred.

Another method was used to create some of the bumpier landscapes, including the setting featuring the wooden arch. These were built using a modular system of tiled sections.

I built a series of square tiles containing various land formations and details that could be rearranged edge-to-edge to form different landscape features. All the surrounding tiles would be linked to the one that is the main focus of the scene.

The ground texture of this main tile could then be set to flow across the others producing a seamless landscape. If required, an infinite ground plane could be added, to extend the distant landscape in all directions.

Modular Landscapes

Some of the landscapes will be produced using
a modular system of tiled sections that can be
rearranged to form various combinations.
Top: *The archwood as a wireframe and*
pre-textured model.

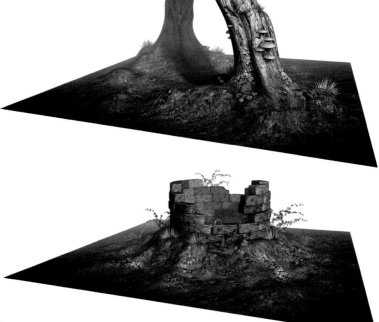

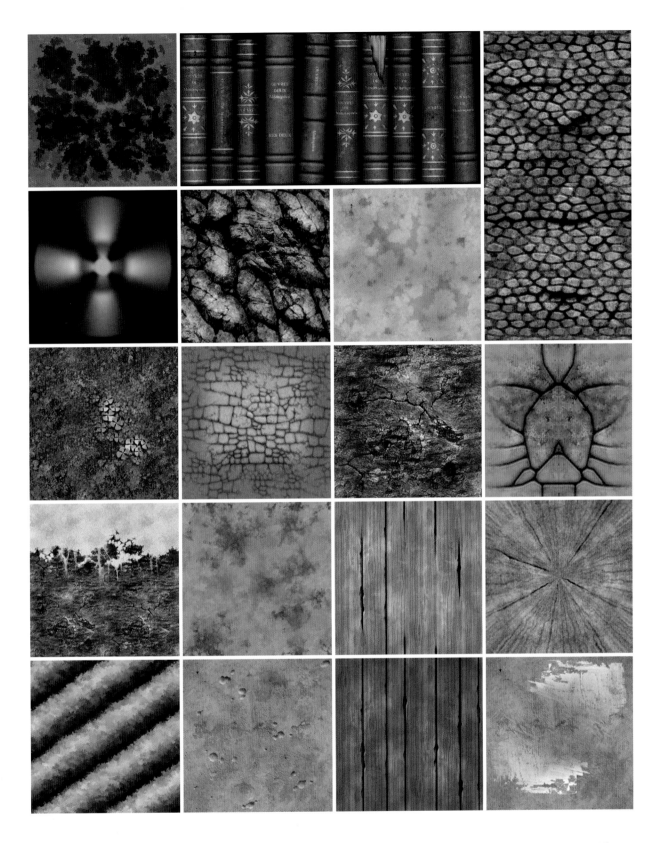

Texture Library

This page: *A small selection of the many textures used throughout the project.*
Opposite page: *The seamless 'archwood' landscape was constructed using the modular method described on the previous page.*

During the course of the project's development I've built up a considerable texture library. Although many of the texture maps are specific to a particular model, there are some that are used regularly throughout the film. For example, I tend to stick to a select few textures for stone surfaces rather than feeling the need to use different ones for each object. This helps to give the film a consistent look throughout. The colour in my scenes is mainly achieved through lighting, preferring to keep the colour of the textures themselves reasonably neutral.

The wooden arch scene was originally built simply as a passing prop for Rustboy to walk under on his first excursion away from home. I quickly posed the character in a sleeping position and sat him under the arch, purely to check the scale of the model. When I saw the result, I immediately felt that the setting deserved a larger part in the film, and it will now be used for one of Rustboy's dream sequences.

The Cliff-Top

Rustboy's favourite spot on the island is a cliff-top looking out to the ocean, as depicted in these original concept drawings and finished 3D scene.

Rustboy's favourite spot on the island is a cliff-top looking out to sea. He has spent many hours here in quiet contemplation, gazing at the rolling waves as they crash against the shore, unaware that this expanse of ocean will become the setting for his greatest adventure.

CHAPTER FIVE

the OCEAN

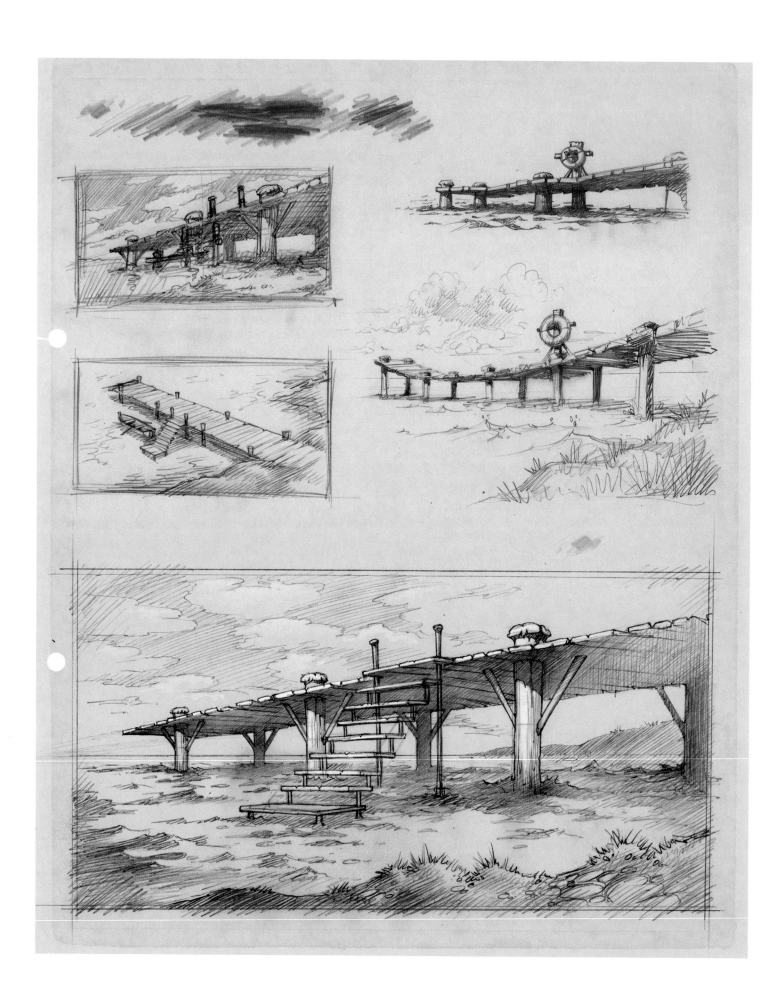

114

THE OCEAN

One day while looking out from his favourite cliff-top setting, Rustboy spots something of interest further along the coast. After venturing down to investigate, it turns out to be a jetty with a small rowing boat tethered alongside. He remembers seeing pictures of this in one of the books in the study, and is eager to try it out. Gathering together some of his belongings, he sets off on his ocean adventure.

After producing a few rough sketches of the jetty, I did some research to figure out the details of how they are normally constructed. I unearthed lots of reference material but none of the examples looked anything like my idea of a jetty, so I decided to stick with my own designs whether they were accurate or not.

Jetty Concepts

Opposite page: *Many quick scribbles were produced to establish the look of the jetty setting where Rustboy sets off on his ocean adventure.*
This page: *Although this design was worked up in colour, the final 3D model would borrow elements from some of the earlier sketches.*

The large picture of Rustboy peering over the edge of the jetty was achieved using a combination of rendered imagery and digitally painted elements. This and many of the other concept images of the ocean sequences represent the look I would ideally like to achieve.

I don't think about the limitations ahead when I'm working out concepts, preferring to set the standard high, and later trying to reach somewhere near that goal. For example, the crashing waves are more complex than I'll ever be able to achieve in the final 3D scene but I will do the best I possibly can.

I spoke earlier of using colour shifts to convey the changing mood of a scene. The jetty setting and the first stage of the boat journey are presented in friendly warm colours to imply that Rustboy is happy and excited at the prospect of this new experience.

As he drifts further out to sea, the colour scheme gradually changes to a cold blue, to signify impending danger.

The main expanse of ocean was achieved using undulating geometry for the large swells, combined with seamless animated texture and bump maps applied across the surface to produce

Building the Jetty

*The various stages in building the finished 3D jetty model.
Digitally painted enhancements were added to the large
image, setting the ideal standard to aim for later.*

Ocean Backdrop

The close-up boat shots will be rendered against a 'rear projection' backdrop of looping pre-rendered ocean footage. This will allow me to concentrate on the waves and splashes around the boat and save on rendering time.

the smaller waves. Additional waves and splashes were created with a combination of geometry, particles, and splashing water footage mapped on to flat planes. One problem I hadn't anticipated was the ocean intersecting and showing inside the boat when viewed from higher angles.

I worked around this by creating a travelling matte of Rustboy and a solid version of the boat to hide the water. This was used to combine separate renders of the ocean footage and Rustboy in the rowing boat at the compositing stage.

For close-ups I used the backdrop technique mentioned earlier, with a pre-rendered ocean loop movie applied to the background plane. Essentially this is the virtual equivalent of the rear-projection system used by Ray Harryhausen and many others to combine new elements with previously filmed footage in-camera. This enables me to concentrate on the boat animation and the splashing waves around it, without worrying about what's going on in the background.

It also helps cut down rendering times considerably. In most cases additional layers of mist and rain will complete the shots, helping to tie the elements together while adding atmosphere.

The further Rustboy ventures out to sea, the worse the weather conditions become. He is struggling to keep balance as the boat is constantly lifted up on the crests of huge waves and smashed

The Rowing Boat

Rustboy was enlarged considerably in comparison to the scale of the boat. This was a case of choosing aesthetics over realism to make the character and rowing boat 'feel' right as a whole.

Ocean Adventure

Above: The 'rear projection' set up for close-ups.
Below: An inspirational concept illustration of the stormy
weather conditions of the later ocean sequences.
Opposite page: Storyboard sequence of the whale
encounter and a concept illustration of the whale's eye.

Whale Encounter

Rustboy is lifted high in the air on the back of a whale in this detailed concept painting.

Danger at Sea

Opposite page: *Rustboy is having trouble staying
inside the boat in this stormy concept illustration.*
This page: *Storyboard panels of the harpoon attack.*

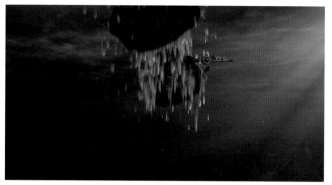

down again. As he clutches the edge of the vessel in an attempt to stop it capsizing, he suddenly finds himself eye to eye with a huge whale. The colossal creature emerges from the water near the boat and dives back in with an enormous splash that knocks Rustboy off his feet.

After a moment of relative calm, it rises up again, this time directly below the boat, lifting it high above the ocean.

The whale crashes into the water causing Rustboy to lose his balance and topple over the side of the boat. He just manages to hang on to the edge, and after a considerable struggle, pulls himself back up, collapsing in the bottom of the boat with exhaustion.

The boat must have been adrift for some time, as Rustboy awakens to find that the storm has settled and he is now sailing in calmer waters. He pulls himself up to the edge of the boat and cautiously peers over the side. Without giving too much of the story away at this stage, Rustboy eventually finds himself at the receiving end of a harpoon attack. The harpoon ricochets off his body with a metallic clunk, knocking him overboard.

The shot of Rustboy plunging into the ocean and sinking to the seabed was created using many different layers. A seamless animated water texture was wrapped around the inside of a cylinder at a large scale. The cylinder was enlarged to encompass the entire scene, and dimly lit to produce a subtle animated wavy background. Rustboy was animated plunging into the water and sinking to the bottom to establish the camera move. The character was temporarily removed and only the cylinder rendered to produce a background movie.

Using the same work-file, a ground plane was introduced and mapped with a suitable texture for the seabed. Another plane was added and an animated wave texture applied to form the water surface. These planes were rendered against black, with fog used to fade the planes off into the distance, resulting in a second movie file. This movie was composited with the background footage using the 'screen' method. Two more layers were produced in the same way to add floating seaweed and light beams to the background movie.

Ocean Plunge

A sequence of movie frames showing Rustboy sinking to the bottom of the sea.

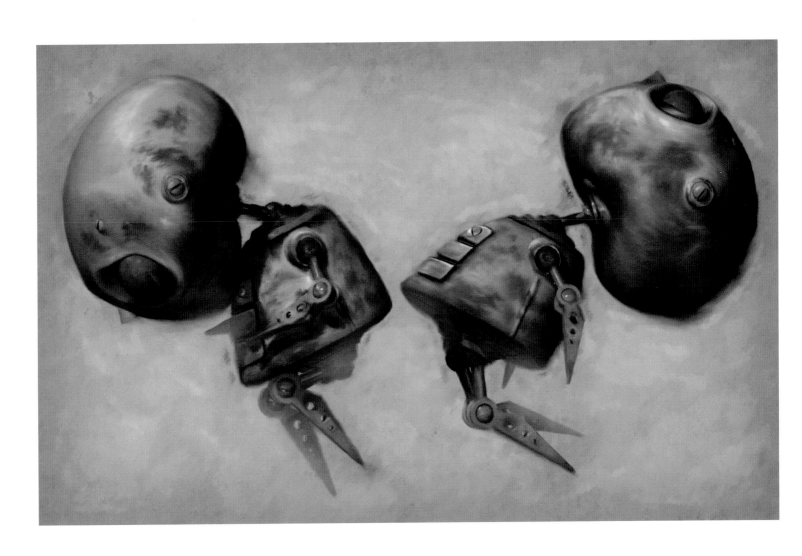

Drowning

Rustboy is given a painterly treatment in this image produced for general promotional purposes.

Underwater Concept

This anchor wreck was one of the first concept paintings produced to establish the look of the barnacle encrusted underwater sequences.

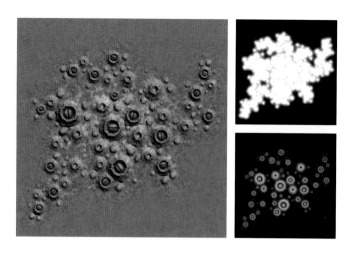

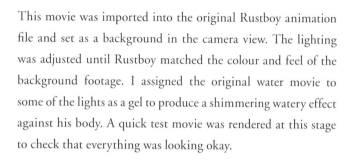

This movie was imported into the original Rustboy animation file and set as a background in the camera view. The lighting was adjusted until Rustboy matched the colour and feel of the background footage. I assigned the original water movie to some of the lights as a gel to produce a shimmering watery effect against his body. A quick test movie was rendered at this stage to check that everything was looking okay.

Barnacle Clusters

I devised a method of adding a layer of barnacles to any existing model regardless of its texture. The objects above show the first test applied to wood and metal.

The next step was to create the bubbles using particles. Several particle emitters were attached to various points on Rustboy's body, and the appropriate properties assigned.

The particles were set to render as polygons and a bubble texture applied. The particle settings required a little trial and error until they acted the way bubbles should. When I was happy with the results, Rustboy, the bubbles, and the background footage were rendered out as one final movie clip.

Motion blur was added to the first few frames in post, as Rustboy plunges into the water, and a little colour correction completed the sequence.

For the underwater sequences I wanted to have the ability to encrust selected objects and areas with clusters of barnacles. I devised a technique for adding the barnacles to any object,

regardless of the existing texture underneath. I began by modelling a selection of 3D barnacles, duplicating and scaling them to various sizes, and arranging the objects to form a cluster. These were rendered out from a top-down view with an alpha channel. This enabled me to paste the cut-out barnacles into a transparent layer in Photoshop over a black background.

I blurred and smudged the edges until they blended smoothly into the black. After loading and saving the selection to create a new soft edged alpha mask, I flattened the image and saved the file. This would be used as the barnacle image map – now I needed a corresponding bump map.

I returned to the 3D barnacle file, applied a black material to all the objects and set a thin layer of white fog from the base to the height of the barnacles. When rendered against a white background this effectively produces a z-depth map. This image was inverted in Photoshop to create the barnacle bump map.

The resulting texture and bump maps could now be added to a new layer in the texture editor, with the alpha channel used to blend it with the underlying texture, and the bump map applied to give the barnacles added depth.

Towards the end of the film, a pirate shipwreck was required to give the coast of the new island a feeling of hostility. I produced a rough scribble of the type of galleon I had in mind from memory, fully intending to look for some reference material to help with the finished design. However, I liked the feel of this initial scamp, and ended up drawing a neater version without seeking further guidance. I worked it through to a full concept illustration using the 'multiply' method mentioned earlier.

Maritime Details

A series of concept drawings of various elements that will be required in and around the ocean sequences.

To reinforce the pirate connection, I dropped the usual 'jolly roger' flag in favour of a skull and crossbones carving on the stern of the shipwreck. The final 3D version of the galleon setting has not been built at this stage but I imagine that I will follow the concept illustration fairly closely in this case.

The artwork in this book includes the majority of the designs produced for the film to date, although I have intentionally omitted a few pieces of work to avoid giving away too much of the story ahead of the film's completion.

These pages represent the closure of phase one of the project, although there is a lot of work ahead as I approach phase two - the animation stage. I feel that I'm well on the way to fulfilling my vow to complete a project, however long it takes. And this has been no ordinary project, having evolved into the largest single body of work I've ever produced by far. There's no doubt that the computer has played a large part in enabling me to finally achieve my film-making ambitions. Things have certainly come a long way since my days of misshapen lumps of modelling-clay and painted toilet rolls.

Pirate Ship Sketches

Opposite page: *The initial quick sketches of the
pirate shipwreck shown here in rough colour studies.*
Above: *A skull and crossbones detail carved
on the stern of the ship.*

Pirate Ship Concept

*The final shipwreck concept painting
was based entirely on the original
five-minute rough sketch.*

STEREOSCOPIC 3D GALLERY

Use the enclosed red and blue 3D glasses
to view the images on the following pages.
For best results, view in bright conditions,
allowing a few minutes for your eyes
to become accustomed to the glasses.

ACKNOWLEDGEMENTS

Thanks to Bobby, Christine, Dave, Doug, Erik,
John and Kenneth, Kathleen and John, Libby, Michael (k10k),
Og, Rich and Jason (pixelsurgeon), Wayne, Zeldman,
3D Total, CG Channel, Cool HomePages, Linkdup,
3D World magazine, CG World magazine,
Digital Studio magazine, Entertainment Weekly magazine,
Jump magazine, and everyone who has supported the
Rustboy project and helped with this book.

Special thanks to Jim Coudal (www.coudal.com)
and Douglas Mullen (www.d-10.net)

3D Glasses supplied by Rainbow Symphony
(www.rainbowsymphony.com)

Images on page seventeen © Storyland Limited 2003

Adobe Photoshop, Adobe After Effects, and Macromedia Flash
are trademarks of their respective owners.